Contents

Chapter 1

Chapter 2

Chapter 3

Chapter 4

Chapter 5

Chapter 6

Chapter 7

Chapter 8

Chapter 9

Final Words

Introduction

We all want to live our lives to the fullest and enjoy financial freedom, don't we? Well, it is indeed a process and cannot be perceived as something that happens overnight. It is important that you define your goals and objectives both short term and long term, paving a well thought out path to achieve them. After attending school for years; being taught the process of working hard and gaining an education in order to achieve your goals it is difficult for most individuals to think outside of the box. These days most companies are outsourcing and off-shoring making the job market stagnant. Who hasn't received a call from their friendly local service company only to discover that the caller is from the other side of the world? In many parts of the world the era of secure job with good pay and conditions is quickly coming to an end which is why it is more important now more than ever that people start seeking financial security rather than job security.

Without the right mindset and priorities financial freedom is not possible. How many people feel lost after they lose their jobs? How many people get overwhelmed when the debts and bills start piling up? Other people who dream about financial freedom buy books about strategies that create wealth; they read the first few pages and jump head first into the first investment they come across. As you would expect, that person invariably fails. The correct mindset is lacking in these circumstances.

The aim of this book is to help equip people who are seeking financial success with the same basic mindset that successful people possess. It is my hope that after reading this book you will acquire a brand new outlook on the path you wish to pursue to your financial success.

Chapter 1

How we think – changing our mindset

Let's be realistic for a moment here! How often can you tell a "wanna-be-rich" person from a financially stable business man? Most times we can. The greatest misconception about being wealthy is that you have to flaunt your wealth to show individuals that you are wealthy. Believe it or not there might be millionaire families on your street and you'd never know it. That's because most millionaires look like regular individuals. They own regular houses and auto-mobiles. They might have a few luxuries but most average millionaires can't be spotted on a daily basis; they prefer it to be that way and don't flaunt their wealth.

Assets or Obligations?

You need to know the difference between an asset and an obligation. Once you can figure this out then you are half way there. An asset puts cash in your pocket without you having to execute much work for it.

A financial obligation is something that takes cash out of your pockets.

A simple example of an asset: if you had $30.000 and used this money for a down payment on a positivity geared house; renting it out if the investment was sound; eventually the tenants would pay the house off for you. Once the house is paid you would have a stream of income, which if managed properly would provide you with an income which would require little or no work to maintain.

A simple example of an obligation is: if you borrowed $30.000 to buy a new car. You would have to pay interest on a car which will cost you money to maintain and will lose value for every year that you own it.

Now that we can differentiate between the two, if you wish to be wealthy you need to acquire as many assets as possible and do away with as many financial obligations as possible. Wealthy people are mostly concerned about educating their youngsters about financial freedom, creating real opportunities and how to make smart informed business decisions.

This is not to rule out the necessity of a formal education but in truth you will not be taught financial skills in school.

Common education primarily teaches people how to be the best employees they can possibly be. Look at the most financially successful people and you will find that many of them are NOT highly educated but rather they will pay educated people to do what they cannot.

Consequently, you need to teach your youngster the real rules of cash and value, and that true education is more than that which is learned in college.

Wealthy people are concerned with producing as much passive revenue as they can ,and working less for earned revenue. This they know will help them to continue getting wealthier and richer. Your goal ought to be to earn as much passive revenue as you potentially can and convert earned revenue from an occupation into passive revenue.

Be open minded

To be open minded means thinking outside of the box and taking a serious look at the results of what you are doing currently as opposed to adopting a totally different approach and its potential results. It is so simple to fight the urge of preconceived notions on a given matter, and listen to the statement or issue presented to you. Think of it as attempting to solve a mystery on TV. The evident answer is rarely the correct one. Reaching the answer involves gathering facts and discarding biases. Let's start shifting the focus, thinking of new ways to earn and the endless possibilities that exist when we think outside the box. It's so simple to be drawn into one way of thinking after hearing another person's ideas so do your best to abstain until you believe that you've solved the issue. Try to think like a youngster. They are so full of life and see the world on a totally different level. Be the optimist. Explore statements. I can't say enough on this matter.

Erroneous statements are made daily and "poor" thinkers take these statements and run. Check out the facts for truth. Believability is everything. Check your facts before you repeat them and you'll gain believability and the respect of other people.

Chapter 2

What We Bring About in Our Lives

No matter what is being said the law of attraction is real! If you've ever seen 'The Secret' then you're probably convinced that it works. I'm sure you are wondering what you are doing wrong since you have a secular job and you are able to pay some of the bills right? You still have a hassle stepping up to anything life changing right? Keep reading....your questions will be answered!

What We Get

It's funny how you can get so much done if you are motivated and on the flip side you don't get much done of you are de-motivated. Your power to manifest your wants directly corresponds to the degree of awareness you have. Keep increasing your awareness. Think and say positive thoughts as these very words are the actions you are affirming in your lives. We all merit everything we ever wanted and much more.

We need to work on our own personalities to ensure that positive energy flows. To evidence cash you must be specific with cash. You must produce and design affirmations about cash and financial abundance. As frequently as you may

think of it, say aloud, or to yourself, "I'm a cash magnet. I merit financial abundance." These phrases and sentences will pick your energy vibrations up to an elevated level, and help to re-train your brain to think about HOW you can get something rather than just be-leave you can't afford it..

Keep speaking positively and keep believing that there are opportunities out there which will come your way. You need to train your brain to recognize these opportunities. Money will not mysteriously turn up on your front porch. That would be unrealistic. You must be prepared to pick up the hints and recognize opportunities when they come your way.

When you start drawing in abundance in little ways it will get simpler to appreciate, have gratitude and draw on matters which YOU see as larger and more crucial.

Cash is cash to the universe, and abundance comes in all forms. This is a great one. This is the one that's working for me. I've studied and read about the Law of Attraction and I recognize that damaging be-gets more damaging and favourable vibration brings abundance. So instead of worrying about the bills and the due date and why they can't be paid, worry about finding the time to do something incredibly profiting so that you can make some cash.

In order to bring about cash, you have to work out your own personal relationship with cash and tweak it. Work out how you feel about cash, if you have any dark and deeply implanted opinions or reactions towards cash, or if you've learned a particular thought pattern regarding cash. Increase your cognisance, recite cash affirmations, and if you are a worrier, simply begin fretting about what the heck you are going to do with all this cash not the opposite. Believe me it works!

Chapter 3

Planning for Success

In order or achieve, or even get to the next level, it is extremely important that you plan the next move or the next step. Don't expect things to happen by chance. If you do you will always be in the same position or worse. Many experts state that being prepared is your most beneficial bet for success.

Readiness comes in a lot of different forms. Take for instance an athlete, he/she gears up his/her body for competition by training, a pupil sets up his/her brain for an examination by studying and a policeman does likewise through intense training. When one's body and brain are correctly prepared, the psychological effect of turning into a winner is greatly heightened. It is also noteworthy that in order to win you have to learn how to lose. There are many valuable lessons that can be learnt. It is significant to remember that losing isn't an indictment of your inability, instead, it ought to be viewed as a learning tool, utilized to better your skills. Simply but also crucially, it's all about establishing an honest set of goals. Your goals have to be achievable and not beyond expectations. Establishing realistic goals is your first step towards determining what to do and where you want to go.

For many, it's easier to remain the same individual you've always been instead of becoming somebody whom other people will hold in elevated regard, envy and even criticize. In order to become a winner, one has to prepare, set goals, acquire a vision and make sure you act.

Chapter 4

Do You Play to Lose or Win?

Back to my point earlier, it all starts with the mindset. You must decide if you play to win or lose. Looking at prominent sports figures Tiger Woods comes to mind when you think of playing to win. But the mentality of a winner goes far
 past the sporting fields of competition; it extends to relationships, family, career, and money. Much of winning is a mental state, a readiness by design that is preplanned in your brain.

In order to succeed at anything in your life you must learn to have a positive outlook and take full responsibilities for the actions and occurrences in your life. Make sure that you understand that failure does not determine your way forward. Get up, brush yourself off and move on. You can't afford to roll over and play dead. Most people who succeed in life have failed so many times before.

It is important to note that you cannot control the changes that take place in the world or the economy but you can control how YOU REACT to these changes and what positive steps you can take to succeed. Success requires you to possess a positive mental attitude and to take full responsibility of your life.

If you tend to blame others for your shortcomings or failure, now is a good time to stop, take a step back and re-evaluate the real problem, trying to nail down the solution. Blaming others can be a very damaging way to go through life. The answer and the real results lie within you!

Remember your true key to success is how you think. No one can change that for you. That is entirely upon you. Please read on and perhaps this will help you to reach your goals or give you the edge you are looking for. People with a winning mentality in any field are active and always looking for ways to improve themselves. They see failure and rejection as temporary obstacles that must be overcome.

If the plan is to achieve something there must be a set of goals or a course of action to take to achieve it. When everything seems to be going against me I remind myself of a quote by Henry Ford *"When everything seems to be going against you, remember an air-plane takes off against the wind, not with it."*

Chapter 5

Don't Dream It, Do It!

A lot of us think about what we want to achieve in life but because we are so busy with our secular job or the other stresses in life we get side-tracked, ending up just dreaming for years. Nothing is put in place to achieve those goals. Evidently, you will never get to point B from point A if you are doing nothing to get there. You are able to achieve any goal if you work at it, trust in yourself and treat every setback as an opportunity to learn and improve. Regardless of what you wish to accomplish, whether it's singing with a rock group, beginning your own business or becoming wealthy, abide by these steps and you will soon be well on your way to the life you've always conceived of.

Are You A Dreamer Or A Doer?

Clear your mind and clearly think about what you want to achieve. Create a time line and put those goals in writing. The first reason that most individuals don't get what they wish for is that they don't *know* what they wish for. Wealthy individuals are totally clear that they want wealth. They are totally dedicated to creating wealth. As long as it's legal, ethical, and moral, they'll do whatever it takes to have wealth.

It is important to filter out the negatives in order to focus. The negatives might mean a neighbour or a friend. Don't listen to the distracting noises around you. Get focused with a tunnel vision. Remain positive. Cast out thoughts of failure from your psyche as soon as they come up. Figure out a plan. Decide on a goal and then work out what you have to do to get there. Do what it takes to get there. Get a time management coach, move to a different city, cut down on the overtime at work which is unpaid. Set small goals and use them as a stepping stone to the getting to the larger goals.

Train your thoughts to think a lot about being successful. Keep your goal on the front burner until you achieve it. Know that some days the road might seem smoother than others. Use the setbacks as a motivation and press on. Remember the saying "Rome wasn't built in a day" and don't quit, even if things appear bleak. Learn from other people. Talk to others who have been through the same roadblocks evaluate their accomplishments and the time they took to get from point A to point B. Read lots of inspirational books, there are many available, from "The Seven Spiritual Laws of Success" by Deepak Chopra to old favourites like "Think and Grow Rich" by Napoleon Hill. Select from a plethora of books to keep you motivated and give you new thoughts. These guys did not step into riches overnight. It took a lot of time and dedication and hard work. Your journey is no different.

Chapter 6
Are You Thinking Big?

Ask yourself the question. "Am I thinking BIG?" Don't limit yourself. It is OK to desire riches. Our culture cannot seem to make up its mind about the value of ambition. We might grow up poor or not so well off but we managed to get through school and get a regular job to stay afloat; that cannot be all there is to life right? What did all the other guys who are well off do in order to get there? In order to settle conflicts about ambition, you have to get a clearer thought of what you truly wish.

How to Expand the Scope of Your Thinking

We spoke earlier about documenting your goals on paper so that they become real. They are no longer a fragment of your imagination but realistic and attainable goals. They are now on your "to do" list and a little of what you do everyday must be bringing you a step closer to achieving them.

Think about what you'd accomplish if you could accomplish anything and didn't have to worry about cash. Write out your purpose in life in one sentence. Try out career counselling or self-help books if you are not certain what you wish to accomplish. Lack of ambition might stem from not having discovered goals that are correct for you.

If you have given up and lost ambition because your goals looked out of the question, you might simply have to organize your work differently.

Ways to help yourself think big include:

• *Getting into the Right Frame of Mind*. It is important that you take life in strides. Think of it as a marathon and not a sprint. That is why we have to set timelines and be cognisant of them. Prioritize your goals and ensure that you work on them every day.

• _Break every job into smaller jobs_. Don't try to accomplish everything today. Break your goals into smaller goals and focus on creating a way to get there. It is never going to happen overnight. If you feel overwhelmed try to take a step back; regroup and focus on one little step at a time. It works!

• _Establishing good habits and resisting bad ones._ This can go a long way towards preventing fatigue. Make changes in your life. Drop the bad habits. Find strategies for staying on track and sticking to achieving your objectives. Instead of going with a pre-determined and hypothetical outcome, focus on your mission step by step. Learn from your successes and failures and take note of your turning points and milestones. It is OK to have doubts and wonder if your plans will work but you cannot allow doubts to take up too much space in your life. Always think positively and reach out to someone to inspire you if you need to.

• _Keep your focus on building your long term momentum._ Always bear in mind that we are working with a process here. Don't expect to get rich overnight or all your plans to materialize right after you outline what they are. Establish good habits and take small steps to get there. It's OK, just breathe!

• _Give yourself permission to be ambitious_. The sky is the limit. We all want to be successful and so need to think of ways to achieve our goal. It is OK to want to desire riches, as we discussed before. There is nothing wrong with being ambitious. Therefore, think of what you want, work hard and accept that it's OK to acquire credit for what you have done.

• _Ask yourself what kind of life you wish to live._ It all depends on what you wish to achieve. Ask yourself the question. Do you wish to lead a productive life, an easy going one or something in between?
The more you get in touch with what you truly want the happier you are likely to be.

Chapter 7

Turn Problems into Opportunity

Have you really taken a step back and thought really hard about the problems we face on a day to day basis? Most of them come as a result of the decisions we make in our lives. At times the bad decisions become real problems years down the line and then we are faced with fixing the problem. It all goes back to changing our mindset. We are less likely to create a disaster when we really think things through, not making hasty decisions, taking some time to think.

Always think of the possible solutions now that the problems are evident. What are you going to do to try to fix this problem? Stressing about the seriousness of the problem doesn't help. Focus on getting real solutions in place. Don't get discouraged. You have heard that a positive mental attitude will better your outlook. Every problem carries its equivalent size of opportunity, however, most people focus on the problem itself instead of the solutions or opportunities these problems can provide. When we focus on the problem rather than the solution we are focusing our energy negatively. Success comes when we turn problems into opportunities. This is all part of using your mind to change how you see your problems. When you see everything as an opportunity, instead of a problem, your focus will begin to shift.

Before you know it, you will begin to experience real, lasting changes that will have a powerful effect on your life and future success. Thinking outside the box and finding real solutions will strengthen your character as you learn to excel in today's difficult economy. There is always a way out. Are you able to find it? Use your brain. The answers are there. You will feel so much better when you overcome these obstacles. It makes so much more of a difference and it makes you stronger.

Chapter 8

Taking a Good, Hard Look at Yourself

Everything we looked at in the previous chapters comes right back to YOU! YOU need to make a decision as to what you want to achieve. YOU need to set the goals and structure the priorities accordingly. YOU need to do something each day that takes you that much closer to your goal. Live for yourself. Once you perpetually attempt to be the person other people wish you to be, you cheat yourself out of individuality and your own aspirations.

Take a really long look at what you wish to accomplish and design a routine which will ultimately lead you to success. Comprehend that even if you can't control outside conditions, you are able to control your response to them. If you are currently working in a job that does not seem to be going anywhere, look at this job as "where you are now" and ask yourself the question: "What I am doing today to ensure that I am not in this position 5 years down the line?" Plan your exit carefully and over time so that when you get there you would have already created an income stream or a better alternative that is guaranteed to work or has already been working over the years. It all leads back to the right timing.

Slow up. If you are constantly pressed to finish tasks, you will develop a damaging mental attitude towards life. If time is a commodity, calculate how you can schedule your chores more efficiently. Simply by getting up 15 minutes earlier every day, you will have the time to say hello to your neighbour, pet a pup or simply gaze out the window at the rain. Learn something new every day and work on your mental attitude. This is extremely important to succeeding in life. Do what makes you happy. Start a new course, take a class, and learn a new language. Whatever will take you way from the routine.

In all your efforts to create a new you with a new mental attitude and new outlook in life, don't be blinded by all your efforts and fail to recognize the persons around you. Help others. Offering a helping hand to those in need makes you feel needed and worthwhile. Make it a habit to volunteer for charitable organizations. Assisting other people allows us to be grateful for the blessings we have and helps us to maintain a favourable mental attitude.

Make sure you hold favourable feelings or vibrations about cash. Remember the "Law of Attraction". Consequently, if you feel favourable emotions when you consider getting cash, you may draw in more cash into your life.

When you see others with cash, feel appreciation for what they have. Each time you get cash, feel great about it and those occurrences will step-up.

Write and speak favourable affirmations. It all begins with the thought process so be careful what you are thinking about because the very same deeds will manifest themselves in our day to day lives. For instance, you may write, "I'm receiving more and more cash each day from the sale of my fresh books and audiotapes." You may likewise speak favourable affirmations. As you continue to write and/or speak favourable affirmations, your subconscious will go on to work to attract the wealth you wish for.

Chapter 9

You Are Who Your Friends Are

You might not have thought about the impact your friends have on you. It is true that in most cases you tend to adapt the mindset of the people you hang out with. If you realize that your friends are negative or they are comfortable in poverty you have to think of planning your exit from that friendship. It is difficult to focus on the goals ahead if the people you spend a lot of time with are impacting on you negatively.

.

Sadly, we need to cut ourselves off from people who are negative thinkers. We have to find and make fresh friends who have already succeeded and have the millionaire mindset. Attend motivational seminars and get acquainted with like minded people. Observe yourself in what you say, do and believe! Are they the actions of a millionaire mentality? If not, then quit and replace with more favourable thoughts and actions. Fake it till you make it!

The subconscious mind doesn't know the difference. Soon your thoughts will afford fresh possibilities.

Everybody has to begin somewhere. Ultimate success has nothing to do with where you were born, who your parents and relatives are and being born with the silver spoon in your mouth scenario. Success starts when you determine where you are now, where you want to be, and developing a plan to get there. Utilize your own God-given intuition and be great. At the same time, we have to be open-minded, acknowledging our own errors and learning from them.

Final Words

I hope that I was able to inspire you through the different scenarios and processes mentioned in this book. I would love for you to challenge yourself; do not settle for mediocrity. The sky is the limit and your ultimate success is based on the amount of work you are willing to put in; placing a time line on the goals you set for yourself. I've always had good mentors in my life who gave me the support I needed when I felt lost or lonely. Find a support system now! It's this support system that keeps you on track; much like a lighthouse keeps ships from crashing into the shore.

Learn to honour the riches you already have in your life. It doesn't matter how much you have in your bank account or if you're living in a alley. You need to first construct a baseline of what you're grateful for and centre on that as a building block to facilitate advancement.

Find what keeps you motivated; maintain tunnel vision regarding what you need to accomplish. Lose the negative friends and colleagues around you and surround yourself with positivity. Produce synergy with all your systems of wealth to acquire more wealth.

I would like to conclude by saying it doesn't matter what position you occupy in life at the moment. The ultimate goal is what matters. Alter or change your thought process and pave a way to get to the goal you have documented for yourself. Always be mindful that it is going to be a process.